POP CLASSICS FOR TWO

Arrangements by Mark Phillips

ISBN 978-1-5400-6534-6

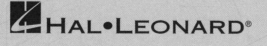

Visit Hal Leonard Online at
www.halleonard.com

Contact us:
Hal Leonard
7777 West Bluemound Road
Milwaukee, WI 53213
Email: info@halleonard.com

In Europe, contact:
Hal Leonard Europe Limited
42 Wigmore Street
Marylebone, London, W1U 2RN
Email: info@halleonardeurope.com

In Australia, contact:
Hal Leonard Australia Pty. Ltd.
4 Lentara Court
Cheltenham, Victoria, 3192 Australia
Email: info@halleonard.com.au

AFRICA

CLARINETS

Words and Music by DAVID PAICH
and JEFF PORCARO

Moderately

Play 3 times

To Coda

2nd time, D.S. al Coda
(take repeats)

CODA

ALONE

CLARINETS

Words and Music by BILLY STEINBERG
and TOM KELLY

Moderately

CAN'T SMILE WITHOUT YOU

Clarinets

Words and Music by CHRIS ARNOLD,
DAVID MARTIN and GEOFF MORROW

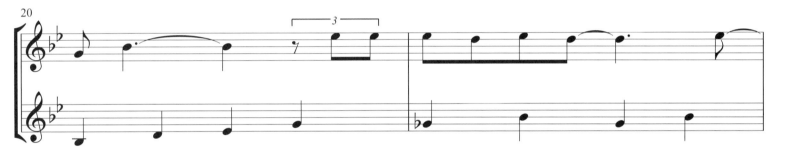

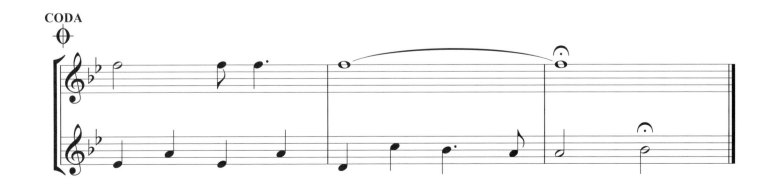

CENTERFOLD

CLARINETS

Words and Music by
SETH JUSTMAN

DANCING QUEEN

CLARINETS

Words and Music by BENNY ANDERSSON,
BJÖRN ULVAEUS and STIG ANDERSON

Moderately

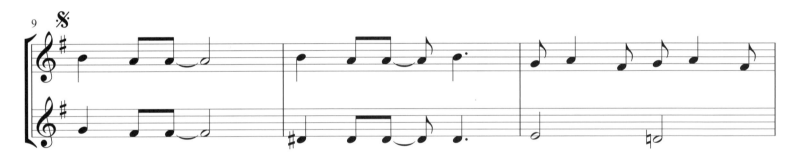

To Coda ⊕

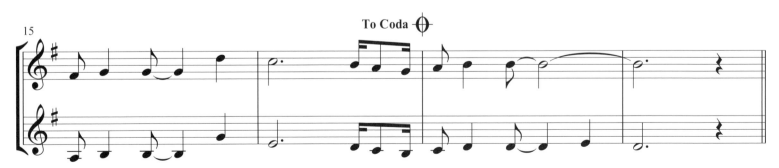

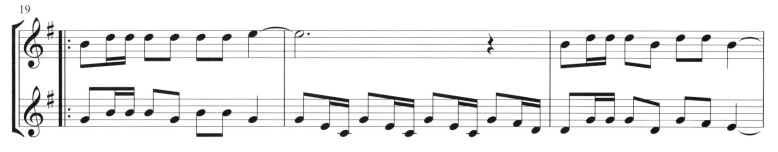

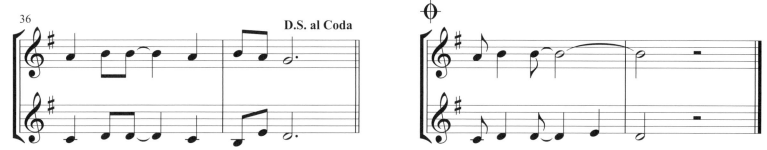

DUST IN THE WIND

CLARINETS

Words and Music by
KERRY LIVGREN

Moderately, in 2

To Coda ⊕

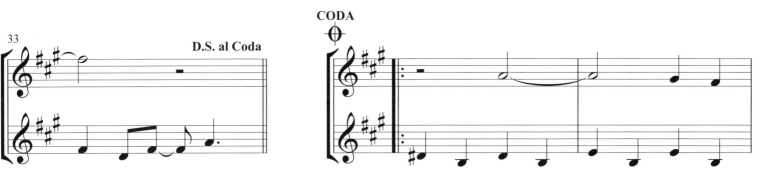

EVERY BREATH YOU TAKE

CLARINETS

Words and Music by
STING

D.S. al Coda

CODA

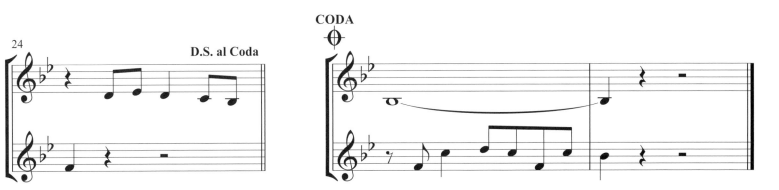

EYE OF THE TIGER

Theme from ROCKY III

Clarinets

Words and Music by FRANK SULLIVAN
and JIM PETERIK

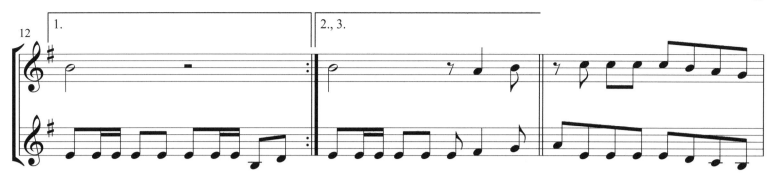

I MELT WITH YOU

CLARINETS

Words and Music by RICHARD IAN BROWN,
MICHAEL FRANCIS CONROY, ROBERT JAMES GREY,
GARY FRANCES McDOWELL and STEPHEN JAMES WALKER

Moderately fast

I STILL HAVEN'T FOUND WHAT I'M LOOKING FOR

CLARINETS

Words and Music by
U2

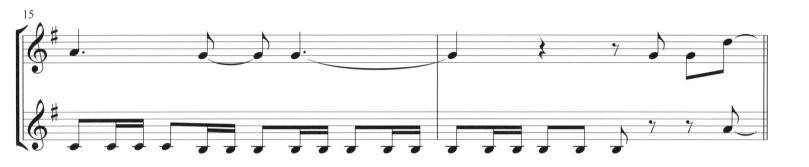

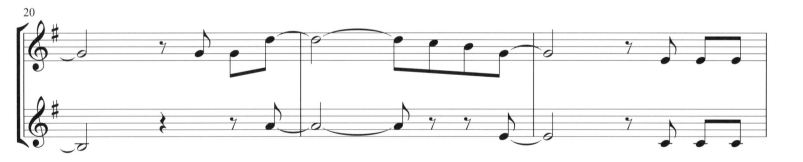

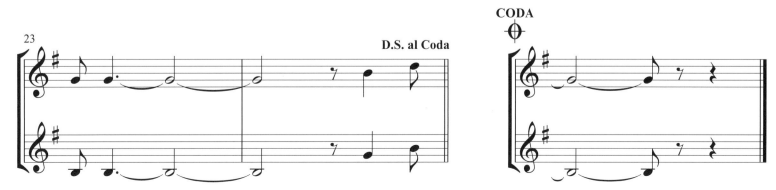

IMAGINE

CLARINETS

Words and Music by
JOHN LENNON

Moderately slow

To Coda ⊕

D.S. al Coda
(take 2nd ending)

CODA

JESSIE'S GIRL

CLARINETS

Words and Music by
RICK SPRINGFIELD

Moderately fast

LEAN ON ME

CLARINETS

Words and Music by
BILL WITHERS

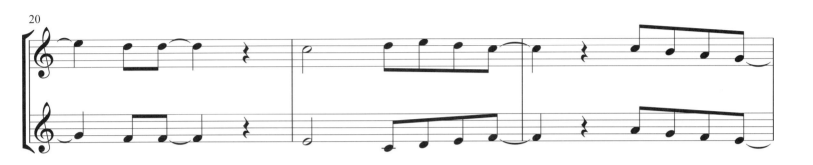

PIANO MAN

CLARINETS

Words and Music by
BILLY JOEL

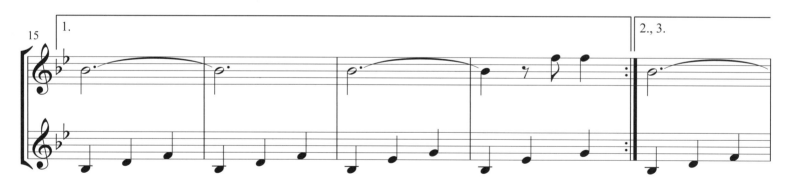

To Coda ⊕   **D.S. al Coda**
(no repeat)

CODA
⊕

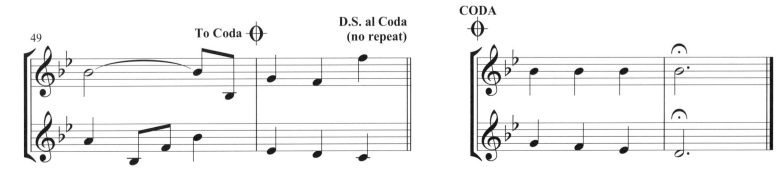

RIGHT HERE WAITING

CLARINETS

Words and Music by
RICHARD MARX

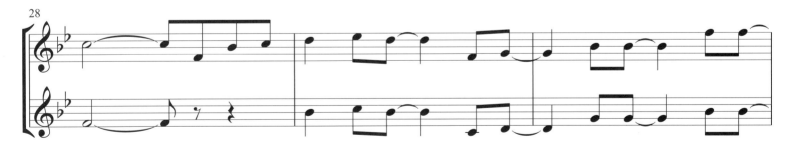

SILLY LOVE SONGS

CLARINETS

Words and Music by PAUL McCARTNEY
and LINDA McCARTNEY

Moderately

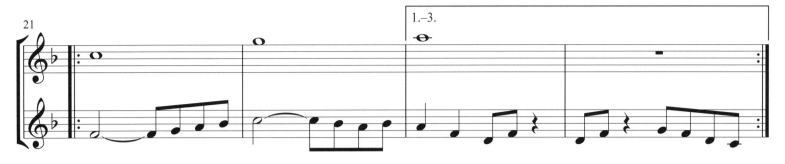

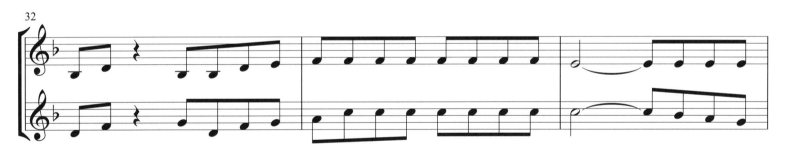

THE SOUND OF SILENCE

CLARINETS

Words and Music by
PAUL SIMON

Moderately

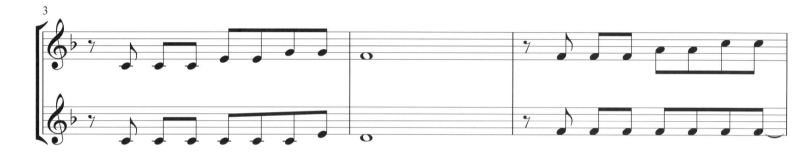

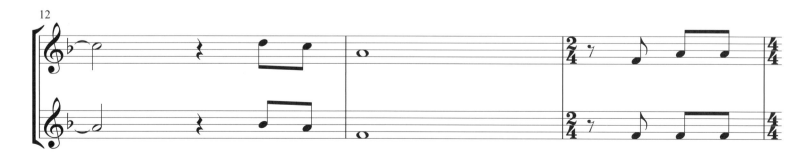

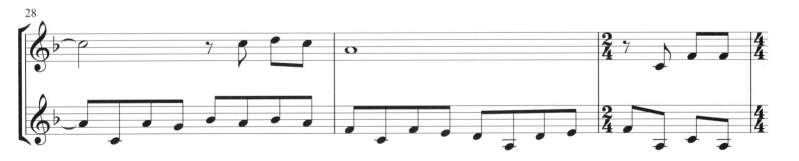

STAND BY ME

CLARINETS

Words and Music by JERRY LEIBER,
MIKE STOLLER and BEN E. KING

Moderately

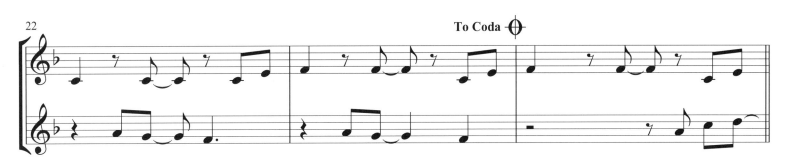

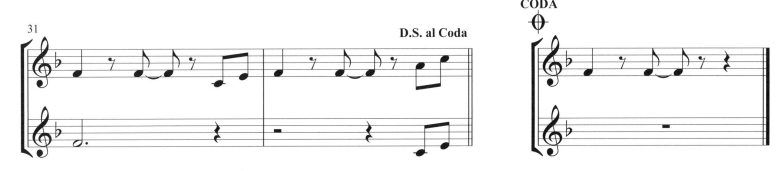

SWEET CAROLINE

CLARINETS

Words and Music by
NEIL DIAMOND

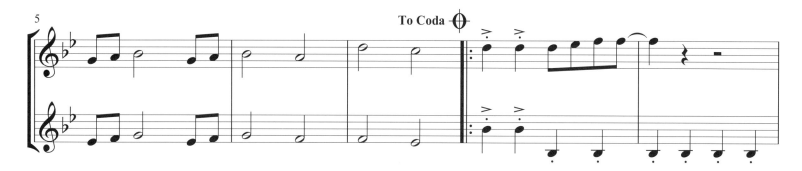

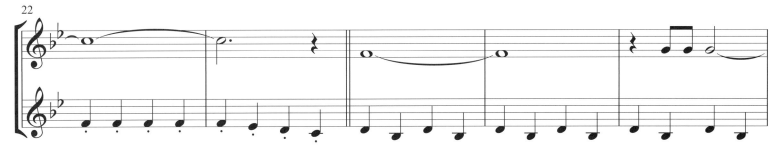

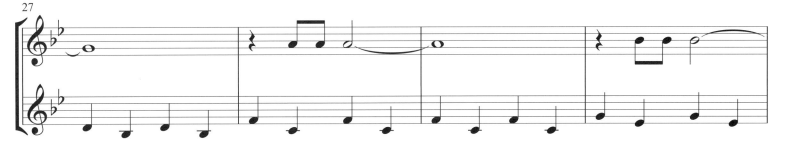

CODA

2nd time, D.C. al Coda

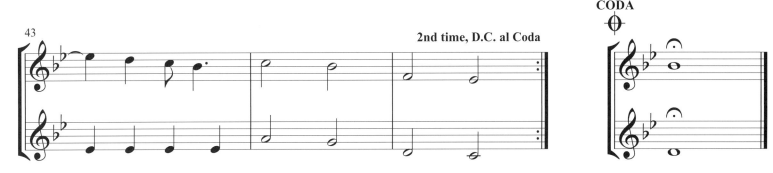

TAKE ON ME

CLARINETS

Words by PAL WAAKTAAR
and MAGNE FURUHOLMNE
Words by PAL WAAKTAAR,
MAGNE FURUHOLMNE and MORTN HARKET

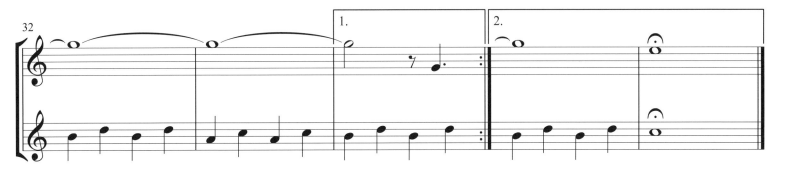

TIME AFTER TIME

CLARINETS

Words and Music by CYNDI LAUPER
and ROB HYMAN

Moderately fast

To Coda ⊕

D.C. al Coda
(take 2nd ending)

CODA
⊕

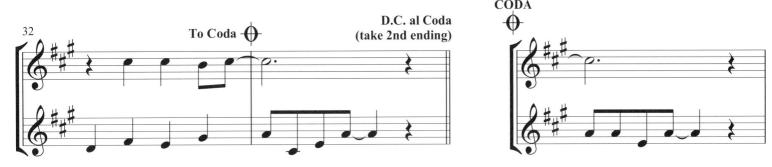

WE BUILT THIS CITY

CLARINETS

Words and Music by BERNIE TAUPIN,
MARTIN PAGE, DENNIS LAMBERT
and PETER WOLF

Moderately fast

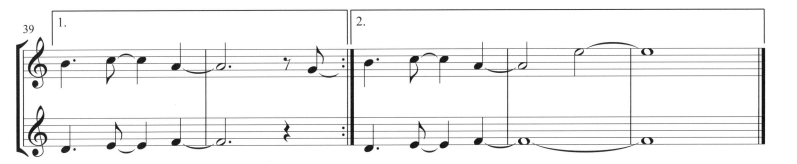

YOU ARE SO BEAUTIFUL

Clarinets

Words and Music by BILLY PRESTON
and BRUCE FISHER

Slowly, with feeling

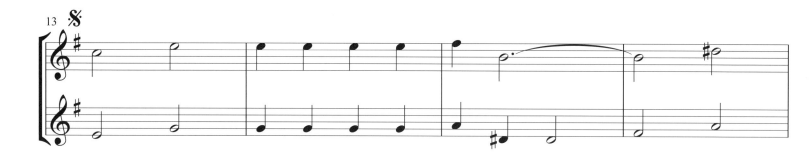

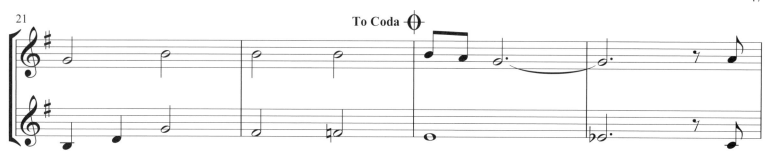

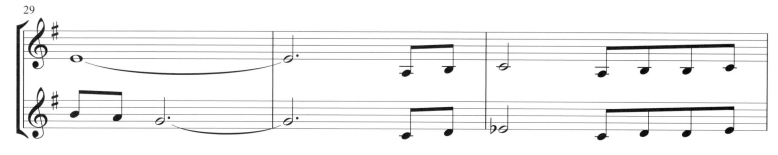

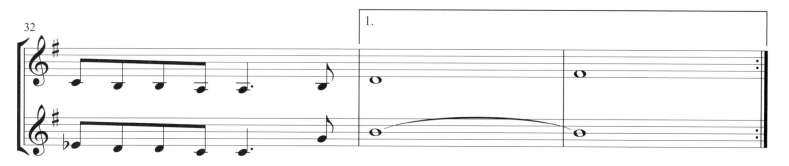